THE COMPI
JUJITSUAN

BY
W. H. GARRUD

WITH A FOREWORD BY
PERCY LONGHURST

THE AUTHOR

PROF. S. K. UYENISHI
From whom Prof. W. H. Garrud acquired the science of Jujitsu,
the wonderful Japanese art of self-defence

Preface

I T seems to be the ambition of every one after having obtained a sound knowledge of a certain art to write a book upon it. I find myself no exception to the rule.

Several books on Jujitsu have been written during the many years since I began to study that fascinating science, and I have been content to read these while supplying my pupils with typewritten instructions of my own system of tuition.

Yielding, however, to the numerous requests of my pupils, both personal and those living in the provinces and abroad, for a complete work in book form, in this volume I now describe all the tricks and methods of self-protection from assault which it has been my good fortune to acquire from such masters as Raku Uyenishi, Yukio Tani, Tarro Myake, and other Japanese experts.

My object in bringing this book before the world is to enable students to have always at hand for reference when desired the methods followed by the above masters of Jujitsu as taught to myself, to enable those who had my typewritten sheets to possess a compact printed work, and to enable others to become possessed of a really complete book of Japanese Self-Defence, such as has not previously appeared.

I have had under my instruction very large numbers of the Special Constables enrolled consequent upon the first war with Germany, who had been strongly advised to learn Jujitsu, and I have also given several Jujitsu displays before large audiences composed entirely of Special Constables.

Finally, I may say that the police forces of Great Britain have fully realized the importance of at least some of their members being trained in this important art, and every encouragement is given to those who are eager to obtain the requisite instruction and practice. I am glad to know that towards the accomplishment of this end I have been able to make a modest contribution.

W. H. G.

Foreword to Seventh Edition

SINCE the fifth edition of this book appeared the author, Mr. W. H. Garrud, has died. Happily, his death did not take place until he had had the satisfaction of realizing that within a few years of the publication of his *The Complete Jujitsuan* the great interest of the police forces in the art he so thoroughly understood had extended in a really remarkable degree to all classes of the athletically minded civil population. Jujitsu today holds a secure position as a foremost system of Self-Defence, and also as a valuable addition to the means of physical recreation and training. It is practised in hundreds of gymnasiums throughout the world, and Jujitsu clubs have come into existence in all parts of Great Britain.

This development has not been confined to Great Britain or even to Europe. In America, Australasia, and particularly in South Africa, there has been an ever-growing and practical interest in the art. This is sufficient evidence of the realization and appreciation of the utility of Jujitsu, of its value as one of the most effective—if not *the* most effective—system of self-defence ever devised.

There is a special reason for this judgment. Knowledge and practice of the art need not—and certainly are not—confined to members of the male sex; to young athletes eager to cultivate and develop their physical powers, to be able to use their strength, agility, and acquired skill towards a definite purpose. Women and girls have been greatly attracted to 'the soft art' because it is one of the main arguments in favour of Jujitsu that the assumed advantages conferred by greater weight and superior physical strength are considerably reduced, if not indeed nullified, when opposed to the antagonistic skill acquired by the well-taught and earnest student of Jujitsu.

Anyone of even under-average weight and muscular power who has the enthusiasm to master thoroughly the principles of Jujitsu, and who by diligent practice becomes expert in their practical application, will be a formidable opponent even if attacked by an aggressor of powerful physique and substantial weight who is ignorant of the art.

It is not merely as a recreation that the British policewoman is given training in Jujitsu.

Moreover, the ability to make effective use of the trained powers of the Jujitsuan is not confined to the 'under thirties'; regular practice of the art is continued by many enthusiasts into the fifth and even sixth decade. I have not yet forgotten the truly extraordinary demonstration given many years ago by Dr. Jigoro Kano, then the highest ranking of the native Japanese leaders of Jujitsu. Although on the wrong side of seventy years, Dr. Kano displayed an activity, a force and astonishing accuracy of balance, movement and timing, that would have been highly creditable in a man of half his years.

Dr. Kano was the devisor of the system of Jujitsu training and instruction to which he gave the name of Judo. His system was adopted by the Japanese military, naval, and police services, since when—outside Japan at least—the use of the term 'Jujitsu' has ceased and the art is commonly known and referred to as Judo.

Boxing and wrestling enthusiasts may not be inclined to agree that Jujitsu—or Judo—as a self-defence art is superior to their own choice, though I believe they would readily admit that neither of these antagonistic exercises is suitable for feminine participation. The question of the comparative merits of the skilled boxer or wrestler and the Judo expert has been debated on innumerable occasions. Usually the disputants 'agree to differ'. Supporters of the western forms of self-defence argue that the Judo expert would quickly fall a victim to a well-planted punch that all his skill would not enable him to avoid and he would be summarily 'knocked out'.

Proof of this assertion is not readily obtainable. It is possible that in a closely confined space the boxer *might* be successful, but not even under these conditions, unless he succeeded in keeping his opponent continuously at arms' length until the quietus was given. Once the antagonists were at close quarters —and this does happen to a couple of boxers playing their own game—the odds seem to be in favour of the Judo expert and his unlimited variety of attacks.

Frequently, too, is it overlooked that the boxer is vulnerable to numerous forms of assault against which his art offers but limited scope for evasion or effective retaliation.

The training and competition rules and regulations of the western boxer and wrestler limit the use of their powers to no small extent. The Judo player's actions acknowledge no such restrictions; his movements are governed by no regulations or rules as to what is fair and unfair. And even the expert in 'rough-housing' and rough-and-tumble fighting might well learn during the course of an all-out encounter with a master of Judo that quite a number of demoralizing and disabling touches familiar to the Judo exponent had escaped his earlier attention.

To appreciate to the full the value of Judo it is essential to realize, and remember, that the art is essentially one of self-protection, its main purpose to ensure its user's safety by putting an aggressor *hors de combat* in the shortest possible time and by the readiest means. What are these means the several sections of this volume—the Standing Defences, the Ground Locks, and Manœuvres, and Jujitsu versus Boxing— indicate clearly enough. At the completion of any individual defence the attacker is left in imminent danger of broken bones or dislocated joints.

I would hasten to add that the Judo aspirant is not advised —very much the reverse—to regard these sections as the most important parts of the book and, therefore, to be given the most immediate and careful study.

Of more than equal importance is that section dealing with the standing throws, Tripping and Throwing. To be able, by means of one of these throws, to bring an assailant to the ground with unexpected speed and shattering force would be sufficient in many instances to 'take all the fight out of him'. Should it not do so, or if it be desirable to prevent the possibility of his working further mischief, then one or other of the limb locks or other disabling tricks may be resorted to.

On *no* account should the Tripping and Throwing section be ignored or studied merely cursorily. In my own judgment it is the most important section of the book. To master the technique of these throws, to be able to use them effectively, accurately and swiftly, to have them at one's finger-ends, is the most important part of the novice's Judo training. That is also the opinion of the native experts. Skill in the use of these throws gives the possessor a self-assurance that is of the utmost value. To have the confidence in one's power to bring down heavily an adversary of much greater bulk and strength than oneself is to be possessed of an asset that is almost a guarantee of the successful outcome of a scrap.

Practise, practise, and practise these standing throws until accuracy becomes all but mechanical. And your time will be well spent. Leave the other sections alone until you are really expert with the throws. Then you may give attention to the 'trimmings'. Many of these, the limb locks and the choke-holds, are hardly possible until the aggressor has been thrown.

It may appear as though undue stress has been given to the disabling locks and holds, and it is a commonplace objection against Judo that the mastery of its actual purpose is not to be acquired except at the cost of risking physical disablement or the equally undesirable danger of inflicting perhaps permanent injury on one's partners in practice bouts.

The answer is that in practices it is perfectly feasible to avoid the above liabilities by keeping one's head and always remembering that the disabling locks, grips, pressures, etc., must *never* be carried to their logical extreme. Again and again the caution is given in the following pages that *never* is a lock or twist to be applied with a jerk. Always pressures and strains are to be applied with a very gradually increasing power. And this must be cut off at once, immediately the other contestant gives the signal.

The writer still has a vivid recollection of the lameness and inconvenience he suffered for several months as a result of the over-enthusiastic vigour with which his partner (a lady) in a demonstration applied a wrist twist. Equally keenly does he recall the more-than-inconvenience resulting from his stupid obstinacy in refusing to accept—until too late—the increasing pain of an arm lock, applied by his instructor, as a warning against continued resistance.

With due care and common sense the possibility of the infliction or the sufferance of physical injury can be safely deferred until some occasion when called upon to defend oneself seriously against attack.

But the opportunities for the use of disabling tricks must not be neglected even during practice bouts. By actual experience and trial one should become sufficiently familiar with their use to be able to apply them with accuracy and despatch should the need arise for serious conflict. When this happens, let there be no half measures; but in friendly contest and practice, prudence must restrain enthusiasm.

I would emphasize the willingness to progress slowly. Judo is not an art to be mastered in half a dozen lessons or as many weeks. When practising a new trick do not leave it until you have reason to believe that the necessary movements come so naturally and in proper sequence in your mind that they are all but automatic. Always remember that half a dozen tricks which you can perform with near-perfection are going to be of more use to you than twenty, each of which has been only partially mastered.

The corollary to this advice is to avoid trying to learn several tricks at the same time.

Even though a creditable exponent of one of the western styles of wrestling, you will find that you have a lot to learn: some things to unlearn. You will be liable to forget, during your Judo initiation, that it is contrary to the fundamental principle of the art that force should be used to oppose force. Judo is the 'gentle or soft art'—the art of giving way, but so that you may gain a tactical advantage. Experience of ordinary wrestling will have informed you that frequently it is judicious to concede ground, to submit to a hold, to allow the initiative to your opponent in order to secure a later advantage. This is the Judo chief principle, though only in the embryonic stage. In Judo the principle is constant. Many Judo tricks, which to the uninitiated appear almost unbelievable, or possible only with the connivance and co-operation of the opponent, are made possible, and effective, only by acting upon this giving-way principle.

I recall a scuffle between a tall, athletic, thirteen-stone man and a little fellow, Judo trained, of perhaps nine stone, a chance encounter on a river-bank. The big chap drove forward, arms and hands outstretched for a devastating grip. The little fellow stood his ground until the other's hands were actually touching him, when he retreated two or three steps. Then, as the grip was actually taken, simultaneously he drew back a foot, stooped, and took a two-handed grip of the attacker's right coat sleeve as he turned about, presenting his back to his assailant. The latter, unable to check his impetus, abruptly rose from the ground and sailed through the air over the other's head, to complete a somersault and drop with a heavy thud beyond the toes of his thrower.

It was a perfect illustration of the Judo principle of giving way and utilizing the antagonist's weight, force, and direction of movement to bring about his downfall.

One item of advice the novice should never neglect when learning a new trick, or indeed whenever he goes on the practice-mat. It is: never sacrifice accuracy to attempted speed of execution. Rapidity is essential to success, but accuracy is even more so. Without complete accuracy—and this includes not only the action of the arms but the movements and placing of the feet and the posture of the body—the effort will be a failure. To these the holds, twists, and thrusts effected by the hands must be regarded as of secondary importance. Perfection of arm work will be wasted if the feet are improperly placed or a wrong inclination given to the body.

Remember: accuracy first. Speed will be developed by constant practice.

Physical make-up matters little, though it will be obvious that certain throws and tricks may come more easily to certain types of physique. The great majority of the native teachers and performers are men on the small side, but I recall that one of the most accomplished British exponents of Judo stands very little short of six feet.

Apart from its undeniable utility, as a means of physical recreation and training Judo ranks high. Not a single part of the bodily framework or the muscles but comes into play and becomes toughened, strengthened, and more enduring. The vital organs obtain benefit; for strenuous as is the exercise, it includes no violent and prolonged strains.

PERCY LONGHURST

May, 1947

Contents

CHAPTER III

TRIPPING AND THROWING

CHAPTER VI

JUJITSU VERSUS BOXING

YUKIO TANI
From whom Prof. Garrud received much training and
valuable practice

General Hints

IN practising the Japanese Art of Self-Defence it is, of course, essential to have an opponent. The would-be Jujitsuan should therefore get a friend who is interested in this sport to practise with him. Either a man friend or a lady friend will do, as this art can be practised equally as well by both sexes, and indeed should be acquired by the weaker sex as being quite as useful to them as to their stronger brothers.

With regard to apparatus it is not absolutely necessary to have anything but the ordinary clothes in which you stand, as of course if attacked you would in all probability be attired so. Therefore you can practise all the tricks and methods contained in this work in ordinary attire.

I should advise you to get from one to eight Japanese Jujitsu mats and a couple of Japanese jackets, and soft shoes.

If, however, you do not desire to go to this expense you can use old coats fastened with a sash round the waist, having first cut off all buttons and sewn up the pockets so as to be certain of having nothing in them which would cause injury when falling. As a substitute for Japanese mats you could make use of a carpet or large rug.

Having obtained the friend, the coats, and the carpet or rug, you are now sufficiently equipped to start.

The best way to learn is to get your friend, whom I will call the assailant or the opponent, to attack you as described in each method. He must use no resistance while you are learning the tricks, but when you have a thorough grasp of them you must get him to attack you in every possible way and use what resistance he likes, and you should then try to defend yourself with the particular method suitable to that attack and as rapidly as possible.

Under no circumstance should you apply any lock with a jerk, otherwise serious injury might result. Every lock should be brought on gently but firmly and with increased pressure until your assailant taps, when you must immediately release him. The signal of defeat is made by tapping with the hand or the foot, and the tap may be made on your body or on the mat or on the victim's own body; in fact on the most convenient and quickest part.

The trips, throws, counters, and the obtaining of the locks can, and should, be made as rapidly as possible, but you must learn to know when to stop; that is, you should stop at the crucial moment of applying the leverage to a joint.

Another hint which should be carefully observed is that the finger- and toe-nails be carefully trimmed to avoid scratching. Also the fingers and toes should not be twisted or forced the wrong way to nature when having a bout, unless you have been so directed in the methods, as one does not wish to have scratches or injured fingers. It will be quite time to suffer these when seriously defending yourself, although your assailant will be the sufferer if you have learnt the methods well.

With regard to the Breakfalls, these are made with either the hands or the feet, according to the particular throw. In some of the throws the Breakfall is made with both hands and feet at the same time.

The Breakfall consists of beating the mat as strongly as possible, and this is only acquired by practice, the palms of the hands or the soles of the feet touching the mat a second before the shoulders or hips, thus avoiding injury to those parts. The arms act as a strong lever or spring, letting the body down gently after the beat. The feet act in a similar manner, but the knees are always well bent, whilst the arms are kept straight, with the exception of one fall, i.e. the forward fall. In this fall the force is broken with the hands and the forearms. The natural instinct when falling forward is to put out the arms and fall on the hands, but this way leads to broken wrists, and is quite against the Japanese idea.

In all Breakfalls the position of the head is very important, and if neglected the head is jerked with more force than is pleasant on to the mat after the fall. Therefore you should take care to always tuck the chin in to the chest in a backward fall, and in to the shoulder when falling sideways. The muscles should be relaxed whilst falling and immediately after the fall, but whilst beating they should be contracted as much as possible, but only momentarily.

When practising the trips and throws, and also when having a bout, the body should be kept upright and the guards made by simply lifting the feet over the assailant's.

In other, or most, styles of wrestling the body is well bent and the legs kept to the rear out of reach, but ordinary wrestling must not be confused with Jujitsu. When Jujitsu is practised as a sport and exercise it is a form of wrestling, and some of the trips and throws are very similar to other styles, but in Jujitsu it is essential for the purpose of keeping a good balance, and also for avoiding being thrown, to keep the body upright, and not to avoid being tripped by getting the legs back. The eyes should also not be allowed to look on the mat or at the assailant's feet. The movements of the assailant's legs can be easily followed by looking at his chest. When well versed in tripping, the Jujitsuan may look anywhere but at the assailant's feet. The Japanese are very strict on this point, or, rather, points.

When doing ground work, i.e. when either one or both combatants are on the ground or mat endeavouring to obtain a lock, each opponent should aim at being near the shoulders or body of the other, and never get near the legs unless trying

c

for a leg lock, and in this case it should only be momentary and sufficiently long enough to obtain the lock. If the attempt fails the position should be abandoned immediately.

On the other hand, each opponent should endeavour to keep his legs between himself and his adversary, the legs being used quite as much as the arms in warding off a lock and getting clear.

Although a great many locks can be obtained by the under wrestler, who has by no means a bad position when he is lying flat on his back, it is advisable to be 'top-dog' as often as possible, as there are more opportunities from this position. There are four standard positions which the top man can take after having thrown his opponent, and from which locks can be obtained, i.e. at the adversary's side with one knee on his body and the other leg outstretched behind. Secondly, sitting on the mat with one side against the opponent's and one arm round his neck. Thirdly, leaning across the opponent's chest with both knees well spread on the mat on one side and the arms on the mat on the other side, chest to chest. Fourthly, sitting astride the opponent with knees on the mat and leaning forward on the look-out for a lock or collar hold. When throwing the assailant one of these standard positions should be obtained according to the throw, but only momentarily, as you must at once attempt one lock or other. During a bout these four positions are constantly being changed until a lock is secured.

With respect to the use of strength or force, it is quite against the principles of Jujitsu, the Japanese art being the 'gentle art', and the strength of the assailant being used against himself. Therefore the methods should be applied with as little force as possible.

When advising the non-use of strength, it must always be assumed that your opponent is stronger and heavier than you. This being the case, it is perfectly obvious that a weaker man pitting his strength against a stronger adversary would be absurd, as the stronger must win in the end.

To use your assailant's strength against himself, you must therefore give way to him: for instance, when tripping, if your opponent pushes you, you must give way and retreat; if he pulls, you must go with him and not make a tug-o'-war of it. When your opponent pushes you, he brings his legs forward and lays himself open to a trip more easily. When he pulls you, you pay attention to guarding and countering, which is quite easy if you have been schooled well in balance.

When on the ground you use your opponent's strength in the same manner, i.e. if he pushes you, give way, if he pulls you, go with him: for instance, if you are in the standard position of leaning across his chest and he pushes you away, go back and fall into a lock, for he will give you his arm in his action of pushing you.

If you are in the under position and your opponent leans forward to obtain the 'Further Bent Arm Lock', assist him over you by pushing his armpit with your free hand.

It will be clearly seen throughout this book how to use your opponent's strength and direction of force against himself.

The illustrations were all taken instantaneously from life, as will be clearly seen from some of the positions which it would be impossible to keep even with the use of props or supports.

CHAPTER I

The Breakfalls

(I) PREPARATORY EXERCISE FOR THE BREAKFALLS ·

Having studied the theory of the Breakfalls in the General Hints we will now proceed to put it into practice.

Lie down at full length on the mat on your back; raise your head, bringing your chin in to your chest; bend your legs slightly so that you can place the soles of your feet flat on the mat. Now roll your body half-way over to your left side, bending your right arm across your chest. (Phase I.)

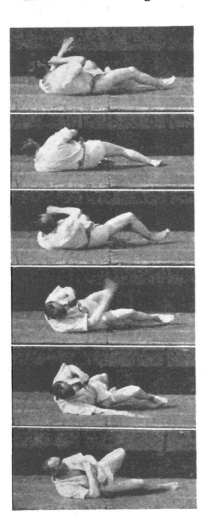

From this position roll your body over half-way on to your right side and beat the palm of your right hand strongly on the mat about ten inches from your side, keeping the arm perfectly straight. (Phases II, III, and IV.)

As you make the beat with the right hand you should bring your left arm across your chest ready for the roll to the left again. (Phases V and VI.)

Repeat this rolling and beating right and left alternately several times, and then rest awhile. It is not advisable to practise too long at this, as it is inclined to make the head ache if done too much at one time.

(2) THE SIDE BREAKFALL

Stand erect in the centre of the mat; raise the right leg forward, keeping it quite straight, and at the same time sink to a squatting position on the left leg. Whilst you are doing this bend your right arm and bring it across the chest ready for the beat on the mat. (Phases I, II, and III.)

When you get to within about four inches of the mat throw the body backward and sideways to the right, and strongly beat the mat on your right side with your right hand a second before your body touches. (Phases IV, V, and VI.)

The head should be kept well raised, and with the chin on the chest and the muscles on the left side of the neck contracted so as to prevent the head from jerking down on the mat after the fall.

Practise this an equal number of times on the other side by squatting on the right leg, raising the left leg, and beating the mat with the left hand.

(3) THE BACKWARD BREAKFALL

Stand erect in the centre of the mat; sink down to the full squatting position, i.e. bending the legs as far as possible, turning the knees and toes outward, keeping the heels together and raising them as you sink.

Raise both your arms straight forward to shoulder height as you sink down. (Phases I and II.)

From this position start the breakfall, sitting down on the haunches, then rolling back on to the shoulder-blades, and beat the hands afterwards to get the proper action of the arms.

When you have practised this well, you must endeavour to make a slight spring from the squatting position backward on to your shoulders, beating the mat a second before they touch. The action is very similar to that of catching a crab in rowing. (Phases III, IV, and V.)

When you roll on your back your legs should shoot up in the air. (Phase VI.)

The last stage of this breakfall should be when you can fall straight back from the attention.

(4) THE FORWARD BREAKFALL
PREPARATORY

Stand erect in the centre of the mat; bend the knees and raise the heels, and sink down to the full squatting position; let the body fall forward, losing the balance, and commence to raise your arms forward. (Phases I, II, and III.)

Continue to fall forward, straightening the legs and thrusting the body forward, but keeping the feet on the same spot, and raise the arms, bending at the elbows. Now beat the palms of the hands and the forearms strongly on the mat, and at such a distance from the feet that when you are at full length your hands are level with your head and about fourteen inches apart, and your elbows just behind your shoulders. (Phases IV, V, and VI.)

No part of your body should touch the mat, and you should rest solely on your forearms and toes.

This should be practised a good deal before you go on to the advanced stage.

(5) THE FORWARD BREAKFALL
ADVANCED

Stand erect in the centre of the mat; lean forward, bending the legs slightly, and then spring upward and forward into the air, raising the arms so that when the body is horizontal they should be in the correct position for the beat.

When the body has attained the horizontal position it should be about three feet above the mat.

When the body has fallen to within about six inches of the mat beat the hands strongly, and immediately afterwards the forearms should come to the mat.

Lower the feet gently to the mat, but keep the body free.

This fall can be led up to by first resting on the hands and feet, and then falling to the mat and beating, then by squatting and falling forward and beating.

(6) THE FORWARD ROLLING BREAKFALL

Stand erect in the centre of the mat; bend forward, and place the hands on the mat about eighteen inches in front of the feet; bring the chin in on the chest and spring over on to the shoulder-blades, carry the legs over the head, and let them fall forward, bending well at the knees, and beat the soles of the feet on the mat.

As you make the beat with the feet you must beat the palms of the hands strongly on the mat at the sides of the body and at a distance of about ten inches.

The spine should be kept well up from the mat, similar to the bridge in ordinary wrestling, until the force of the fall is broken with the hands and feet.

When well practised in the above you should endeavour to do this breakfall by making a kind of forward somersault, alighting on the shoulder-blades a second after making the beat.

(7) THE OBLIQUE FORWARD ROLLING BREAKFALL

Stand erect at one corner of the mat with the left leg forward and the left shoulder in advance. Bend forward and place the left hand on the mat a few inches in front of the left foot and a few inches to the right, with the fingers pointing to the right. At the same time place the right hand on the mat near the left hand, but with the fingers pointing to the front.

Slowly lower the left elbow to the mat; turn the head so that the chin touches the right shoulder, and then spring over on to the left shoulder-blade, rolling obliquely across the back to the right hip, and crossing the left leg over the right and beating the sole of the left foot and the right hand on the mat.

Rise with the impetus of the roll to a standing position, facing the opposite way to which you started.

Do not attempt to rise at first when learning this, but remain at full length.

(8) THE CART-WHEEL BREAKFALL

Stand erect at one corner of the mat with feet apart about twelve inches, and left arm raised straight above head, and the head turned to the left.

Bring the left arm and body down sideways, springing off the left foot, and place the left hand flat on the mat about eighteen inches to the side of the left foot.

Wheel over to your left, bringing the right hand down on the mat about fourteen inches from the left hand, then bring the right foot down, and assume the erect position facing the same way in which you started.

The arms and legs should have a position similar to those of the spokes of a cart-wheel as you go over, and you should go exactly sideways.

This trick is used as an alternative to the breakfall for the Stomach Throw, thus saving you going down on your back.

It is also used in getting to your opponent's head when he is lying on his back with his feet up, preventing you getting near him.

CHAPTER II

The Standing Defences

(1) DEFENCE FOR RIGHT HAND GRIP ON RIGHT WRIST

Your assailant seizes your right wrist with his right hand.

Immediately sink your body a little, bending the right arm, and seize his wrist with your right hand. (Phases I, II, and III.)

Straighten up and turn your body to your right, swinging your left arm over his right upper arm, at the same time pulling on his wrist to keep the arm straight. (Phases IV and V.)

Now slip your left forearm under his elbow joint, and grip your own coat so as to keep your arm in position, and then press strongly down on his wrist, and you will have the lock. (Phase VI.)

This is called the Come Along Hold, by which you can take a man out of a room or to a police-station, or wherever you desire.

The alternative to this lock, when your opponent prevents you, is given farther on in this book.

Practise this an equal number of times on the other side.

(2) DEFENCE FOR LEFT HAND GRIP ON RIGHT WRIST

You are standing facing your assailant, and he seizes your right wrist with his left hand.

Immediately place your left hand upon his left wrist, gripping his wrist with your knuckles upward; raise his arm in a line with your shoulder, then bend your right arm, bringing your elbow down and towards your assailant's body, and press your wrist strongly against his thumb joint, thus forcing his hand inward towards his forearm, whilst your left hand must press his wrist towards your right wrist.

Press firmly, but not with a jerk, until your assailant taps the signal of defeat.

This is a lock upon the thumb joint, and if done with a jerk will break the thumb.

Practise this an equal number of times on the other side by getting a friend to hold your left wrist with his right hand.

D

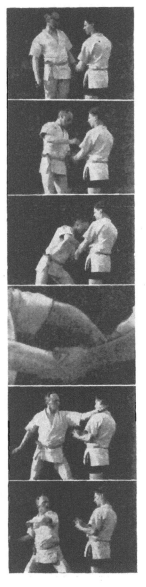

(3) DEFENCE FOR A TWO-HANDED GRIP ON LEFT WRIST

Your assailant seizes your left wrist with both hands. Quickly bend over and grip your own left fist by making a cup of your right hand. (Phases I, II, and III.)

Pull your left wrist up against his thumbs, the weakest point of resistance, swinging your body well back, and bringing your left hand over your right shoulder with the hand open and the fingers straight. (Phases IV and V.)

Straighten your left arm, swinging it forward, and strike a blow at your opponent's neck with the edge of the hand. (Phase VI.)

The hand should strike the neck just below the ear on the carotid artery. If done with force this will knock a man down and unconscious.

The Japanese always strike with the edge of the hand, and they practise striking a stick or piece of wood for the purpose of making the edge of the hand hard.

(4) DEFENCE FOR A GRIP ON EACH WRIST IN FRONT

Your assailant seizes your wrists in front, one· wrist in each hand. Quickly seize his left wrist with your left hand; take a small step backward with your right leg, and push your right arm vertically down, at the same time screwing it inward, thus making your forearm act as a kind of wedge, bringing pressure to bear upon his thumb, the weakest point of resistance. (Phases I, II, and III.)

Having broken the first grip, bring your right leg up again and give his right thumb joint a sharp jab with the heel of your right wrist, compelling him to release his grip on your left wrist. You must do this jab with your right hand open and the fingers inside, so that you can immediately seize his wrist. You now have the grip on his wrists, your arms being crossed. (Phase IV.)

Quickly draw his right arm over his left arm, until the elbow joint reaches the crook of his left arm, then press down on his right wrist with your right hand, and upward on his left wrist with your left hand, thus giving you a powerful lock upon his right elbow joint. (Phases V and VI.)

(5) DEFENCE FOR REAR GRIP
ON EACH WRIST

Your assailant seizes your wrists, one in each hand, from behind. Immediately make a right-about turn, gripping his left wrist with your left hand, and bending your left arm, bringing it behind your back. (Phases I and II.)

Place your right foot on your opponent's left instep, sinking down on your left leg close to your heel. Keep your right leg perfectly straight, and pull him over your right foot on to his left shoulder. (Phases III, IV, V, and VI.)

Immediately after sinking on left leg, you must sit on your haunches, and roll back, and to your left side on to your shoulder-blades.

As soon as you have thrown your adversary, you must release your grip on his left wrist, and rise to your feet facing him, ready to assume one of the standard positions preparatory to obtaining an arm or leg lock.

Practise this an equal number of times on the other side by turning to your left-about and seizing his right wrist with your right hand, and sinking on to your right heel.

(6) DEFENCE FOR HIGH LEFT HAND GRIP ON RIGHT WRIST

Your right arm is bent across your chest. Your assailant seizes your right wrist with his left hand. Immediately place your left forearm over his left wrist and your left hand under your right elbow, whilst your right hand rests on your left biceps, very similar to the act of folding the arms. (Phases I, II, III, IV, and V.)

Hold his hand firmly between your forearms and take a step backward with your right leg, at the same time bending your body forward and sinking on your right knee. (Phase VI.)

The effect of this movement is to force your assailant's left hand backward on to his own forearm, thus securing a wrist lock.

If this is done with a jerk, the result would be a broken wrist.

Practise this an equal number of times on the other side by getting your opponent, with whom you are learning the tricks, to grip your left wrist with his right hand, then transpose the movements explained.

(7) DEFENCE FOR RIGHT HAND GRIP ON THROAT

Your assailant seizes you by the throat in front with his right hand. Immediately lean back a little, raising your right hand, and grasp the little finger edge of his hand, raising your right elbow well up to get a good grip. At the same time grasp his right wrist with your left hand, obtaining a good under grip by keeping your elbow down and inward. (Phases I, II, and III.)

Now slightly lower your head and body to your right, rotating his arm, and raising your left elbow and lowering your right elbow, then suddenly make a right-about turn, slipping your left arm over his upper arm, and passing your left leg round to the other side of your right leg, so that the legs do not get crossed and so that you get a good base on which to stand. (Phase IV.)

Grip his right upper arm firmly under your left armpit, and arch your back, leaning your weight well upon his elbow joint, then force his wrist upward and outward to your left, and you will have obtained the arm lock. (Phases V and VI.)

During the whole process from taking the grip of his wrist you must not change or alter the grips of your hands on his wrist.

Practise this an equal number of times on the other side by getting your opponent to grip your throat with his left hand, then make all the movements described above, but transposed.

(8) DEFENCE FOR TWO-HANDED GRIP ON THROAT

Your assailant seizes you by the throat with both hands in front. Immediately place your right forearm between his wrists from above, and slip your right wrist under his right wrist. Close your right fist, and push it upward and over to your right with your left hand, at the same time turning your head to your right, thus breaking the grip on your throat. (Phases I and II.)

Immediately the grip is broken open your right hand, and, turning the palm away from you, seize his wrist with a firm grip.

Place the little finger edge of your left hand, palm facing you, under his triceps muscle, and with a screwing movement push up and round on this muscle, at the same time turning his wrist round until his elbow joint is pointing away from you and your opponent has been compelled to almost turn his back on you. (Phase III.)

Now quickly slip his forearm over your left forearm, and bend his arm until his hand is forced up along his spine, then quickly take your right hand away from his wrist, and transfer it to his elbow joint, which you push downward, thus levering his arm up behind his back, and giving you a very effective shoulder lock. (Phases IV, V, VI.)

At the moment of pushing down on his elbow you must place your left leg in front of his right leg, to prevent him turning.

(9) DEFENCE FOR LEFT HAND GRIP ON RIGHT LAPEL

Your assailant grips the right lapel of your jacket with his left hand. Immediately raise your right arm and place the bone on the inside of your wrist on your opponent's left hand, screwing the bone into the back of his hand just where it joins the wrist.

Now raise your left arm and take hold of your right hand, the palm of which should now be facing upward, and with the combined strength of both hands press your adversary's hand firmly against your chest. (Phases I, II, III, and IV.)

Bend your body forward and stoop down, your head being slightly inclined to your right, to avoid knocking it against that of your opponent. (Phases V and VI.)

The result of this movement will be to force your assailant's hand backward on to his own forearm, producing a wrist lock which will enforce immediate submission.

Practise this an equal number of times on the other side by getting your opponent to grip your left lapel with his right hand.

(10) DEFENCE FOR A RIGHT HAND GRIP ON RIGHT LAPEL

Your assailant grips the right lapel of your jacket with his right hand. Immediately turn to your right, bringing your chest in contact with his arm. Raise your right arm and grip his wrist with your right hand, your elbow being well raised and your thumb upward. (Phases I and II.)

Swing your left arm up under his right arm and grip the farther lapel of his jacket with your left hand, taking care to place your arm under his elbow joint. (Phases III, IV, V.)

Now press forward and downward strongly with your left arm on his elbow joint, whilst you hold his wrist firmly towards your right shoulder until your assailant submits. (Phase VI.)

Practise this an equal number of times on the other side by getting your opponent to grip the left lapel of your jacket with his left hand.

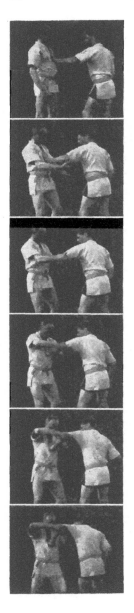

(11) DEFENCE FOR AN OPEN HAND
PUSH ON CHEST

Your assailant places his open hand on your chest and gives you a push. Immediately raise your arms and place your right hand under his elbow joint, then place your left hand under your right hand. (Phases I, II, and III.)

Now lift your opponent's elbow joint well upward and outward, at the same time pulling his arm in to your chest firmly, to prevent him slipping his hand away. (Phase IV.)

Lean your chest forward a little as you lift his elbow, and you will have a wrist lock by which it is possible, if done with a jerk, to break the wrist. (Phases V and VI.)

Practise this an equal number of times on each side by getting your opponent to push you with either hand.

If your opponent pushes you with both hands you must ignore one. When you have obtained the lock on one wrist your opponent's other hand will be useless.

(12) DEFENCE FOR LEFT ARM REAR THROAT GRIP (A)

Your assailant grips you round the throat from behind with his left arm.

Immediately raise your arms, and grasp his left jacket sleeve with your left hand and his elbow with your right hand. (Phases I, II, and III.)

Bend well at your knees to get well under your opponent, then bend your body forward, and take a step forward with your left leg, lifting your opponent right on to your shoulders, then throw him completely over your left shoulder to the mat in front of you. (Phases IV, V, and VI.)

Practise this an equal number of times on the other side by getting your opponent to throw his right arm around your throat, then transpose the movements above described.

(13) DEFENCE FOR LEFT ARM REAR THROAT GRIP (B)

Your assailant seizes you round the throat from behind with his right arm, and pushes you in the small of the back with his left fist, thus pulling you back and preventing you defending yourself with the method just described.

Immediately raise your arms and grasp his right wrist firmly with your left hand, at the same time grip his right elbow with your right hand. (Phases I and II.)

Make a left-about turn, bending your body well, and force your head away from his grip by pulling on his wrist and pressing his elbow downward. (Phases III, IV.)

As soon as your head is free, slip your left forearm under his right forearm, keeping his arm bent at an angle until your left hand rests on his shoulder.

Continue the pressure on his right elbow, and slip your left leg in front of his right leg to prevent him turning away, and you will have the shoulder lock. (Phases V, VI.)

Practise this an equal number of times on the other side by getting your opponent to grip you with his left arm.

(14) DEFENCE FOR LEFT ARM REAR THROAT GRIP (C)

Your assailant seizes you round the throat from behind with his left arm, the wrist of which he holds in his right hand for the purpose of preventing you from withdrawing your head.

Grasp his elbow with your left hand and his wrist with your right hand, and make a right turn of your body, bending well at the waist. (Phases I, II, and III.)

Quit your grasp on his wrist, and place your right arm round his waist from the rear, and grip the sleeve of his jacket. (Phase IV.)

Raise your right foot and jab the back of his right knee with the sole, pulling him backward to the mat. (Phases V and VI.)

As a rule your assailant will release his grip on your head as he falls. If he does not, you can compel him to do so by gripping his left wrist again, and pushing his elbow from you, and secure an arm lock by forcing his arm up his back, or you can get a wrist lock by placing your right hand on his left knuckles, and forcing his hand into his forearm.

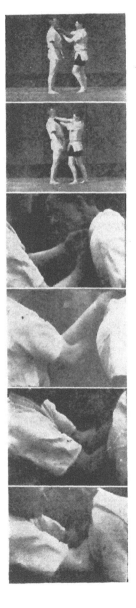

(15) THE CROSS COLLAR HOLD

You are standing facing your assailant. Quickly raise your arms, crossing the left under the right, and with your palms upward.

Slip the four fingers of each hand under his jacket lapels. (Phase I.)

Do not grip his jacket lapels, but reach back as far as you can until your thumbs almost meet at the back of his neck. (Phase II.)

Now grip his jacket lapels, and press the outside bones of your wrists into the sides of his neck just below the ears where the carotid arteries are situated, and pull your assailant's head towards you. (Phases III, IV, and V.)

In the large pictures the right wrist is under the left, but this can be done either way.

————————

This Collar Hold can be done in exactly the same way when you are astride your assailant on the mat.

(16) DEFENCE FOR CROSS COLLAR HOLD

Your assailant attempts to obtain the Cross Collar Hold upon you (Phase I.)

Before he has secured the grip on your jacket lapels raise your arms and place your right hand on his left elbow and your left hand under his right elbow. (Phase II.)

Now pull down on his left elbow with your right hand, and push up on his right elbow with your left hand, at the same time stepping round with your left leg. (Phase III.)

Continue to step round with your left leg, placing your left foot down on the mat, and slipping your hips under him, and pushing his right elbow farther up. (Phase IV.)

Lean your body forward, and bring your left arm over his right arm, but without taking your hand away from his elbow, and commence to lift him with your hips. (Phase V.)

Give a sharp jerk up with your hips and a hard pull on his left elbow, and throw him over your left hip to the ground in front of you. (Phase VI.)

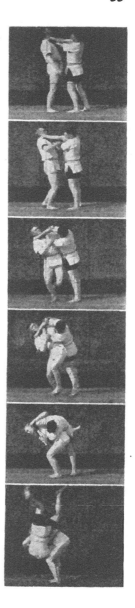

(17) DEFENCE FOR LEFT HAND REAR GRIP ON COLLAR

Your assailant seizes your jacket collar from behind with his left hand and pulls you back. (Phase I.)

Immediately make a left-about turn, so as to face him, and grip his wrist with your right hand, at the same time placing your left hand on his shoulder. (Phases II and III.)

Raise your left leg, and bring it forward to the outside of your opponent's left leg, giving the back of his left knee a vigorous back-kick, at the same time pulling round on his wrist with your right hand and pushing round in the same direction with your left hand, throwing your adversary to the mat in front of you. (Phases IV, V, and VI.)

When throwing your opponent, your body should be bent forward slightly at the waist.

Practise this an equal number of times on the other side by getting your opponent to grip your collar with his right hand.

If, when you turn, your opponent's left leg is to his rear and out of your reach, you may induce him to bring it forward by taking a step backward.

(18) DEFENCE FOR FRONT BODY GRIP UNDER ARMS

Your assailant seizes you round the waist under your arms from the front.

Raise your left arm and push his head back by placing the heel of your wrist under his chin. While you are doing this place your right arm under his left elbow joint.

As soon as you feel his grip breaking take your hand away from his chin and place it on his left shoulder, and at the same time place your right hand on the top of your left wrist, back uppermost.

You are now in the position to bring in the arm lock. Press up under his elbow joint with your left forearm, and at the same time hold his upper arm firmly against your side, to prevent any play being given to it. You now have a very punishing arm lock.

Another way to break his grip is to place one hand under his chin and the other on the back of his head, and twist his head round until he releases you, when you can proceed to obtain the arm lock.

Practise this an equal number of times on each side by pushing his chin with the other hand, and obtaining the lock on his other arm.

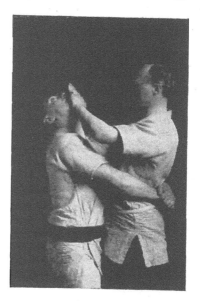

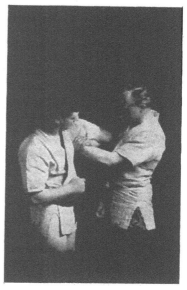

E

(19) DEFENCE FOR FRONT BODY GRIP OVER ARMS

Your assailant seizes you round the waist over your arms from the front, pinioning your arms tightly to your sides. (Phase I.)

Work your hands a little to your front, and dig your thumbs into his groins above the pelvis bone and on each side. By a little experimenting on your own groins you will discover the exact position.

The dig in the groins will compel your assailant to draw back his hips a little, sufficient to enable you to turn your hips. (Phases II and III.)

Bend your knees and turn your hips well round under your opponent's stomach, and at the same time place your left arm round his waist from the rear, and take a hold upon his left jacket sleeve or elbow with your right hand. (Phases IV and V.)

Straighten your legs, lifting your assailant clear of the mat, bend forward and sideways, and throw him over your left hip to the mat in front of you. (Phase VI.)

Practise this an equal number of times on the other side by turning your hips the other way, and throwing him over your right hip.

(20) DEFENCE FOR REAR BODY GRIP
UNDER ARMS (A)

Your assailant seizes you round the waist under your arms from behind. (Phase I.)

Immediately step sideways, so as to bring your opponent's nearer leg between yours. In the illustrations the adversary's left leg is the one forward. (Phase II.)

Stoop down and quickly seize his ankle with both hands, and give a sharp pull up, bringing his leg high up between your own legs, at the same time press backward with your hips, throwing your opponent down backward to the mat. (Phases III, IV, and V.)

Retain your hold upon his ankle, and place the inside of your left knee against the outside of his knee, and force his leg sideways, thus producing a side strain upon his knee joint, and obtaining a leg lock. (Phase VI.)

Instead of pressing his leg sideways when you throw him, you may at once sit upon his knee with your whole weight, pulling up hard upon his ankle meanwhile.

Practise this an equal number of times by getting your opponent to place his other leg well forward.

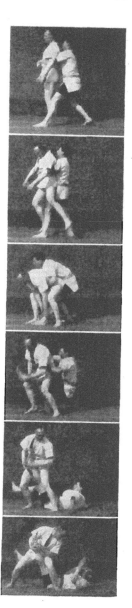

(21) DEFENCE FOR REAR BODY GRIP UNDER ARMS (B)

Your assailant seizes you round the waist under your arms from behind. (Phases I and II.)

Assuming that your adversary has hold of his right wrist with his left hand, hold his right upper arm firmly to your right side with your right arm, taking care to place your elbow behind his elbow, to prevent him withdrawing his arm. (Phase III.)

Give his right knuckles a sharp jab with the heel of your left wrist, causing it to relax, then press his wrist inward towards his forearm, and you will be able to break his wrist quite easily. (Phases IV, V, and VI.)

You can add to the force of the lock, if necessary, by placing your right hand on his right hand after the jab, and so force his wrist inward with the combined efforts of both your hands.

Practise this an equal number of times by getting your opponent to grip his left wrist with his right hand, whereupon you get the lock upon his left wrist.

If your assailant interlaces his fingers, in this grip, pull one finger away till the grip breaks, then seize one of his hands by placing both your thumbs along the back, and the fingers along the palm, then turn round and face him, twisting his arm and forcing his hand back towards his forearm. Method No. 26 gives this wrist lock.

(22) DEFENCE FOR REAR BODY GRIP OVER ARMS

Your assailant seizes you round the waist over your arms from behind, pinioning your arms to your sides. (Phase I.)

Work your hands a little to your rear and dig your thumbs into his groins, as in method No. 19. (Phase II.)

As soon as your assailant has drawn back sufficiently, turn your body to your right, placing your right arm round his waist from the front, at the same time withdraw your right leg clear of his legs, and instantly place the knee at the back of his left knee, jabbing it, and causing it to collapse. (Phases III, IV, and V.)

These combined movements with the arm and leg will cause your opponent to fall backward to the mat. (Phase VI.)

As your adversary falls you must swing round to your right, and assume one of the standard positions preparatory to securing an arm or leg lock.

Practise this an equal number of times by turning to your left and throwing him over your left leg.

(23) THE TRUSSED ARM LOCK ATTACK

Your assailant is standing facing you at arm's length.

Step forward and slightly to your left with your left leg, at the same time raising your arms, and grip his right elbow with your right hand on the outside, at the same time placing the little finger edge of your left hand against his wrist. (Phase I.)

Now pull his elbow towards you, and slip your left hand under his arm and on to his shoulder, at the same time stepping back and round with your right leg, and turning your body to your right. (Phases II, III, and IV.)

Press down strongly on his elbow joint with your right hand, lever up on his forearm with your left forearm and step in front of his right leg with your left leg, and you will have a very effective lock upon his shoulder joint. (Phases V and VI.)

In the last phase you will see the position of the arm in the lock, the picture being enlarged for this purpose.

Practise this an equal number of times on the other side.

(24) THE WRIST AND ELBOW LOCK

Your assailant is standing facing you at arm's length. (Phase I.)

Step forward with your right leg, raising your arms, and grip the outside of his left elbow with your right hand, at the same time placing your left hand over the big knuckles of his hand and gripping them firmly. (Phases II, III, and IV.)

Now raise his arm level with his shoulder, and bend his wrist inward towards his forearm, whilst you hold his elbow firmly to prevent slipping. (Phases V and VI.)

Practise this an equal number of times on the other side by transposing the movements above described.

In the last phase you will observe the opponent about to tap in submission.

The opportunity to do this lock frequently happens when you have your opponent on the mat on his back.

If you place your body against his elbow and then slide your right hand under his arm and substitute your right hand for your left hand you can take away your left hand and hold him with one hand. This is very useful if you are a special constable and wish to blow your whistle for assistance.

(25) THE OUTWARD HAND TWIST THROW

Your assailant is standing facing you at arm's length.

Step forward with your right leg and to the left side of your opponent, at the same time seizing his left hand with your right hand, so that your thumb presses in the back of his hand and your fingers go along his palm. (Phases I and II.)

Immediately you have obtained the above grip, step back with your right leg, turning your body to your right, and raise his arm in a line with your chest, all the while twisting his hand over and outward to your right. When his arm is on a level with your chest raise your left hand, and take a similar grip on his left hand with your thumb on the back and your fingers round the little finger edge of his hand. (Phases III and IV.)

Now throw your opponent with a quick twist to your right, immediately bring his elbow to the mat, and press his hand in towards his forearm, giving you the lock. (Phases V and VI.)

(26) THE INWARD HAND TWIST LOCK

Your assailant is standing facing you at arm's length.

Step forward and slightly to your right with your left leg, at the same time seizing his left hand by placing your left hand over and round the little finger edge, your thumb going on the back of his hand, and your fingers along the palm. (Phases I, II, and III.)

Now step back with your left leg, raising his arm to the level of your shoulder, and taking a similar grip with your right hand round the thumb edge of his hand with your thumb pressing in the back of his hand, and your fingers along his palm, his arm being twisted over and inward as you step back. (Phases IV and V.)

Continue to twist his wrist over to your left side, and force his hand inward towards his forearm, and you will have the lock. (Phase VI.)

Be careful not to push his arm, but to give your attention to his hand.

Practise this an equal number of times on the other side.

(27) THE ALTERNATIVE TO THE COME ALONG HOLD

Your assailant is standing facing you at arm's length, and you have endeavoured to obtain the Come Along Hold by seizing his left wrist with your left hand, and turning round to his left side, swinging your right arm over his upper arm, with the intention of bringing your right forearm under his elbow joint, and holding your own wrist for the lock.

Your assailant has pulled his arm in, bending the elbow, and frustrated your intention. (Phases I and II.)

Immediately turn, facing him again and slipping your right arm over his left arm and your left hand on to his knuckles, then place your right hand on your wrist, and bend his wrist inward towards his forearm and a little outward from his left shoulder, and you will be able to throw him to the mat with a steady pressure, or to break his wrist if done with a jerk. (Phases III, IV, and V.)

In the large picture you will clearly see how the arms and hands are placed, the hold being reversed, to show how it is done on the other side. (Phase VI.)

CHAPTER III
Tripping and Throwing

(1) THE OUTSIDE ANKLE TRIP

We now come to the trips and throws. In self-defence and assuming that your assailant is not using his fists or that you have failed to obtain a standing arm lock, you can very often throw your opponent by catching his coat and jerking him forward or sideways and tripping him.

Apart from self-defence, the trips and counters play an excellent part as one of the best exercises that can be followed.

As a rule both combatants take hold before commencing to trip. This can be done by holding the sleeve or the coat lapel, or one hand on a sleeve and the other on the coat lapel. We will assume that you both take hold of the collar with the left hand and the sleeve with the right hand. (Phase I.)

Your opponent brings his left foot forward; take a step backward with your left foot and place the sole of your right foot against the outside of his left ankle, pushing his leg across to your left, and pulling his left shoulder to you with your right hand. This upsets him and he will be thrown on his back in front of you, where you can follow up with an arm lock.

(2) GUARD AND COUNTER FOR OUTSIDE ANKLE TRIP

Your assailant attempts to trip you up by the Outside Ankle Trip.

As his right foot touches your left ankle lift it quickly and unresistingly over and with a side movement of your knee, i.e. do not lift your knee straight up, thus giving your opponent an opportunity of catching hold of it with his hand.

As soon as your left foot is clear, place the sole against the outside of his ankle, pushing his leg across in front of you, pulling on his jacket with your left hand, and throwing him to your left side by the same trip as he intended to throw you, but with your left leg.

Another counter is to place your left foot firmly on the mat, and as your adversary goes to trip you, quickly raise your right foot and throw him by the same trip.

Practise this an equal number of times on the other side by getting your opponent to make the attempt with his left foot.

(3) THE INSIDE ANKLE TRIP

Take hold of assailant's jacket lapel and sleeve, as explained in the previous method.

Start walking back with your right foot, and, as your opponent walks forward with his left foot, place the sole of your left foot against the inside of his left ankle, and sweep his leg outward, causing him to make a wide straddle. At the same time push him over backward to the mat on his back, and quickly step round to his side and assume one of the standard positions.

You may follow with a leg lock immediately after the throw by catching his left leg under your right armpit, so that your forearm comes under his leg near the ankle, then grip your right hand with your left hand, and lean your body back, thus bringing a great pressure on the soleus muscle.

Step on his right thigh as soon as you have thrown him.

Practise this an equal number of times on the other side by transposing the movements.

(4) GUARD AND COUNTER FOR INSIDE ANKLE TRIP

Your assailant attempts to trip you up by the Inside Ankle Trip.

As his left foot touches the inside of your left ankle, quickly lift your left foot over, and immediately bring your left knee to the outside of his left knee and just behind it, then give a sharp back-kick, at the same time pulling sharply backward with your right hand on his coat sleeve, and throw him by the Cross Hock down to the mat in front of you.

Practise this an equal number of times on the other side by getting your opponent to attempt the trip with his other leg, and then transpose your movements.

(5) THE OUTSIDE CROSS HOCK

Take hold of assailant's jacket lapel and sleeve as before.

As your assailant walks forward with his right foot, step back with your right foot, and as his left leg comes forward, bring your left leg across to the outside of his left leg and place your knee at the back of his knee, then give it a sharp back-kick, at the same time pulling on his jacket sleeve in a backward direction with your right hand, and throw him round and down to the mat in front of you.

You may hook your left leg as you throw him, and you should be careful to bend forward a little at the same time.

As soon as your assailant reaches the mat, you must assume one of the standard positions preparatory to securing a lock.

Practise this an equal number of times by getting your opponent to walk the other way, then transpose your movements.

(6) GUARD AND COUNTER FOR OUTSIDE CROSS HOCK

Your assailant attempts to throw you by the Outside Cross Hock.

As soon as you can conceive what your opponent is about to attempt, place your left foot firmly on the mat with all your weight on it, quickly raise your right leg, and jab the back of his right knee with the sole of your right foot, pulling sharply to your rear with your right hand on his jacket sleeve at the same time, and your opponent will be thrown to the mat in front of you, where you must immediately assume a standard position.

Practise this an equal number of times on the other side by getting your opponent to attempt the throw with his right leg, when you must transpose the movements described above.

F

(7) THE INSIDE CROSS HOCK

Take hold of assailant's jacket lapel and sleeve as before.

Your assailant starts walking forward and to your right side with his right leg. As he does so you must take a step backward with your left leg, and as he brings his left leg round, bring your right leg between his legs, with your right knee against the back of his left knee. (Phases I, II, and III.)

Make a hook of your right knee, and pull his leg well out to your right, at the same time pulling sharply with your right hand, then push him backward and down to the mat on his back. (Phases IV, V, and VI.)

Step smartly back out of reach of his legs, and assume a standard position, or do the Cart-wheel to his head.

Practise this an equal number of times on the other side by getting your opponent to walk the other way, then transpose your movements.

(8) GUARD AND COUNTER FOR INSIDE CROSS HOCK

Your assailant attempts to throw you by the Inside Cross Hock.

As your opponent brings his right leg between yours, quickly raise your leg and give his left leg a sharp jab at the back of the knee with the sole of your left foot, at the same time sharply pulling him backward with your left hand on his jacket, and throw him to the mat in front of you.

Practise this an equal number of times on the other side by getting your opponent to attempt this throw with his left leg, then transpose the movements described above.

The pictures illustrating this counter are opposite to the throw, i.e. left-leg throw instead of right-leg.

(9) THE KNEE TRIP

Take hold of opponent's jacket lapel and sleeve as before.

Take a step obliquely sideways and to your left rear with your left leg, at the same time giving your opponent a slight pull on his left jacket sleeve with your right hand, which will induce him to step round with his left leg. (Phases I and II.)

The instant he is about to do this, raise your right leg and place the sole of your right foot against the outside of his left knee, and a sharp pull downward and to your rear with your right hand will throw him down to the mat in front of you. (Phases III to VI.)

Practise this an equal number of times on the other side by transposing your movements.

(10) GUARD AND COUNTER FOR THE KNEE TRIP

Your assailant attempts to throw you by the Knee Trip.

As he raises his right leg, swing your left leg over his foot with a slight spring from your right foot, and making a right turn of your body. (Phases I, II, and III.)

Immediately sink down on your left heel and extend your right leg, placing the sole of the foot against the outside of his left ankle, and pulling sharply downward and to your rear with your right hand on his jacket sleeve. Roll back on to your shoulder-blades, throwing your opponent over your extended leg on to his left shoulder. (Phases IV to VI.)

Instead of rising, you can roll round to your right, swinging your left arm round his neck, into the standard position ready for the Cradle or other lock.

Practise this an equal number of times on the other side by getting your opponent to attempt to throw you with his other leg.

(11) THE ANKLE ROLL

Take hold of assailant's jacket lapel and sleeve as before.

Take a step obliquely sideways and to your left rear with your left leg, at the same time giving your opponent a slight pull on his left jacket sleeve with your right hand, which will induce him to step round in that direction.

The instant he is about to bring his left leg forward extend your right leg and place the sole of your foot against the outside of his ankle, at the same time sinking down close to your left heel and pulling sharply with your right hand on his jacket sleeve. He will then be thrown over your extended leg to the mat.

You may rise immediately or you may roll round into the standard position preparatory to getting the Cradle Lock.

Practise this an equal number of times on the other side by transposing the movements described above.

(12) GUARD AND COUNTER FOR THE ANKLE ROLL

Your assailant attempts to throw you by the Ankle Roll.

As he raises his right leg, swing your left leg over his foot, and place your left foot on the mat near his right shoulder. (Phases I to IV.)

Immediately swing your right leg over his body with left turn of your body, at the same time seizing his left wrist. Place your right foot down on the mat about ten inches from his head, and force his left elbow joint against your left thigh, thus obtaining a very effective arm lock. (Phases V and VI.)

Practise this an equal number of times by getting your opponent to attempt to throw you with his other leg, whereupon you transpose the movements described above.

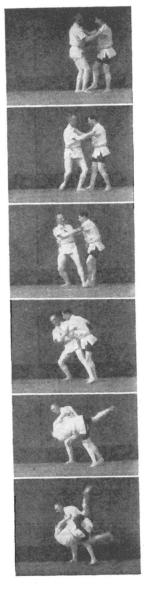

(13) THE SIDE PULL OVER

Take hold of assailant's jacket lapel and sleeve as before.

Take a short step backward with your left leg, at the same time giving your opponent a slight pull on his jacket sleeve with your right hand, to induce him to step forward.

As your opponent brings his left leg forward, quickly make a backward step behind your left leg with your right leg, pointing your toes well outward and turning your body to your right, then immediately extend your left leg right across his legs, so that your left foot comes to the mat just on the outside of his left foot, and pull sharply down and to your right with your right hand, throwing him on to the mat in front of you, where you assume a standard position ready for a lock.

Practise this an equal number of times by transposing the movements described above.

———

Another way of doing this throw is to sink on your right knee as you extend your left leg to throw your opponent.

(14) GUARD AND COUNTER FOR THE SIDE PULL OVER

Your assailant attempts to throw you by the Side Pull Over.

As he turns and extends his left leg to throw you, step over his leg with your left leg, following immediately with your right leg, and slipping your right arm round his waist. Place your right foot down on the mat close to your left leg, bend both legs well, and slip your hips under him; then straighten your legs, bend your body forward, and throw him completely over your right hip to the mat in front of you, where you can instantly assume a standard position.

Practise this an equal number of times on the other side by getting your opponent to attempt to throw you over his other leg, whereupon you transpose the movements described above.

(15) THE SHOULDER THROW

Take hold of your assailant's jacket lapel and jacket sleeve as before.

Give your assailant a slight pull with your right hand on the sleeve of his jacket, to induce him to step forward, and as his right leg comes forward make a step backward and behind your left leg with your right leg, pointing your toes well outward. Then step round with your left leg, bringing the foot near to your right foot, bending well at the knees and passing your left elbow to your right, then raising it and lifting your opponent's left arm so that you can get your left shoulder under his arm close to the armpit. (Phases I to IV.)

Your back should now be close to your opponent's chest and your body well sunk down. Now press back with your hips against his thighs, then straighten your legs and lurch your body forward, throwing him completely over your left shoulder to the mat in front of you, where you immediately assume a standard position ready for a lock. (Phases V and VI.)

Practise this an equal number of times on the other side by transposing the movements described above.

(16) GUARD AND COUNTER FOR SHOULDER THROW

Your assailant attempts to throw you by the Shoulder Throw.

As he turns his body to get under you, place your right hand against his left hip and push it away, thus preventing him from getting close to you, and at the same time weakening his balance. Get your weight firmly on your right leg, raise your left leg with a turn of your body to your right, and throw him by the Cross Hock previously described.

Practise this an equal number of times on the other side by getting your opponent to attempt to throw you on the other side.

(17) THE HIP THROW

Take hold of assailant's jacket lapel with your right hand, and his right sleeve with your left hand.

Step back with your left leg, pointing your toes outward and turning your body slightly to your left, at the same time giving a slight pull on his sleeve with your left hand, to induce him to step forward. As his left leg comes forward, bring your right leg across in front of you and to the other side of your left leg, and place your foot close to your left foot, at the same time turning your body farther round, so that your back comes against his chest. As you turn you must slip your right arm round his body. (Phases I to IV.)

Now bend forward, straightening your legs, and throw him over your right hip to the mat in front of you, where you assume a standard position ready for a lock. (Phases V and VI.)

Practise this an equal number of times on the other side by transposing the movements described above.

(18) GUARD AND COUNTER FOR THE HIP THROW

Your assailant attempts to throw you by the Hip Throw.

As he turns to get under you, push his right hip away from you with your right hand, slip your left arm round his body, and step in front of him and throw him with the Hip Throw, pulling well round with your right hand on his jacket.

Practise this an equal number of times on the other side by getting your opponent to attempt the throw over his other hip.

———

This throw may be done without slipping the arm round your opponent's body, but by retaining your hold upon his jacket, as in the Shoulder Throw.

(19) THE SPRING HIP THROW

Take hold of assailant's jacket lapel and sleeve as in the Ankle Trip.

Step back and behind your left leg with your right leg, pointing your toes well outward, and getting your weight well balanced on that leg. At the same time give your opponent a slight pull with your right hand on the sleeve of his jacket. (Phases I and II.)

As he steps forward with his left leg, raise your left knee, place the lower part of your leg right across his thighs, lever him up with the combined efforts of your arms and leg, and throw him over your left thigh to the mat in front of you, where you immediately assume a standard position ready for a lock. (Phases III to VI.)

Practise this an equal number of times on the other side by transposing the movements described above.

(20) GUARD AND COUNTER FOR SPRING HIP THROW

Your assailant attempts to throw you by the Spring Hip Throw.

As he turns and raises his leg, push his hip away from you with your right hand, and swing your left arm round his neck, slipping your hips under him, then throw him over your left hip with a sharp pull on his jacket with your right hand, immediately assuming a standard position ready for a lock.

Practise this an equal number of times on the other side by getting your opponent to attempt to throw you over his other leg.

(21) THE SIDE STEP SWEEP

Take hold of assailant's jacket lapel and sleeve as in Ankle Trip.

Make a step sideways to your left with your left leg, at the same time slightly pulling your opponent's right sleeve with your left hand to induce him to step to his right, then as your opponent draws his left leg up to his right, place the sole of your right foot against the outside of his left ankle, and push it to your left, at the same time giving a good lift up with both your hands, then pull sharply downward with your right hand, throwing him to the mat in front of you.

Practise this an equal number of times on the other side by transposing the movements described above.

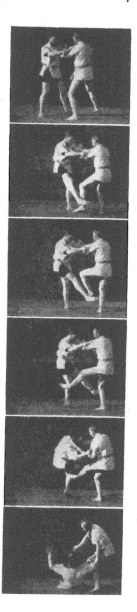

(22) GUARD AND COUNTER FOR THE SIDE STEP SWEEP

Your assailant attempts to throw you by the Side Step Sweep.

As he brings his right leg up to trip you, lift your leg quickly over, and place the sole of your foot against the back of his left knee, giving his jacket a sharp pull to your left and downward, and throw him to the mat in front of you, where you assume a standard position ready for a lock.

Practise this an equal number of times on the other side by getting your opponent to attempt the throw on the other side.

G

(23) THE SCISSORS

Take hold of assailant's jacket lapel and sleeve as in Ankle Trip.

Knock his right hand away from your lapel with your left forearm, and turn your body to your left, getting as much as possible to his left side, but at arm's length. (Phases I and II.)

Quickly place your left hand flat on the mat near your left foot, at the same time bringing your right leg forward, and placing the foot down just in front of your opponent's left foot. (Phases III and IV.)

Now swing both your legs up sideways, so that your right leg comes across the bend of his waist and your left leg across the back of his knees. Then give a sharp pull on his sleeve with your right hand in a backward direction, and roll your body round on to your shoulder-blades on the mat, throwing your opponent flat on his back. You can follow this up by applying the leg lock under the armpit described farther on in this book. (Phases V and VI.)

Practise this an equal number of times on the other side by transposing the movements described above.

(24) GUARD AND COUNTER FOR THE SCISSORS

Your assailant attempts to throw you with the Scissors.

As he throws his legs up across yours, quickly step over his rear foot with your right leg, and sink on to your right knee, at the same time seizing his foot with your right hand and wrapping your left arm round his leg, so that your forearm comes under the muscle just below his calf. Then place your left hand upon your right wrist and press his toes downward, whilst you press up with your left forearm, and you will have a very effective leg lock.

Practise this an equal number of times on the other side by getting your opponent to attempt to throw you on the other side.

(25) THE STOMACH THROW

Take hold of assailant's jacket lapel and sleeve as in Ankle Trip.

Make a backward step with your right leg, slightly pulling your opponent towards you. (Phase I.)

Now raise your left leg, and place the sole of the foot against his stomach, at the same time bending both legs and sinking to the mat close to your right heel. Immediately roll back on to your shoulder-blades, and straighten your left leg, and pulling hard on your opponent's jacket, and kick him right over your head on to the mat on the other side of your right shoulder.

You can immediately rise to your feet, or you can, with the impetus of your roll, bring your legs and body over him, and get to the astride standard position, where you can try for the Collar Hold or the Splits.

Practise this an equal number of times by throwing him with your right leg.

(26) GUARD AND COUNTER FOR THE STOMACH THROW

Your assailant attempts to throw you with the Stomach Throw.

As he raises his left leg to place his foot against your stomach, seize his heel with your left hand, drawing his leg across to your left side. Then quickly raise your right leg, and place the sole of your foot against the back of his right knee, giving it a sharp jab, and pulling hard on his jacket sleeve downward and to your rear with your right hand, throwing him down on to the mat in front of you, where you can assume a standard position ready for a lock.

Practise this an equal number of times on the other side by getting your opponent to attempt the throw with his other leg.

CHAPTER IV

The Ground Locks

(I) THE FOOT ON CHEST ARM LOCK

Your assailant is lying flat on his back on the mat, and you are standing by his left side close to his armpit. (Phase I.)

Stoop down and seize his left wrist with both hands and raise his arm, getting your weight well on your right leg. (Phases II and III.)

Pull your assailant's arm up straight, and raise your left foot and place it on his chest close to his armpit. (Phase IV.)

Draw your assailant's arm across your shin-bone, so that his elbow joint comes against the bone, and then press his wrist backward, at the same time bending your left leg and pushing your shin-bone against his elbow joint, and you will have the Arm Lock. Observe the opponent about to give the signal of defeat by tapping his right hand on the mat. (Phases V and VI.)

(2) THE STRAIGHT ARM LOCK BETWEEN THIGHS

Your assailant is lying flat on his back on the mat, and you are standing on his left side with your leg close to his body. (Phase I.)

Seize his left wrist with both hands, and pull his wrist up to your waist, getting your weight well on your left leg. (Phase II.)

Sink to the squat on your left leg, bringing your haunches close to your left heel, and make a semicircle with your right leg round and over his head. (Phase III.)

Continue circling your leg until it is over his throat and almost straight at the knee. (Phase IV.)

Sink on to your haunches and throw yourself flat on your shoulder-blades at right-angles to your opponent, then bring his elbow joint over your left thigh, clutching his arm with both thighs, and press down on his wrist, and you will have the Arm Lock. (Phases V and VI.)

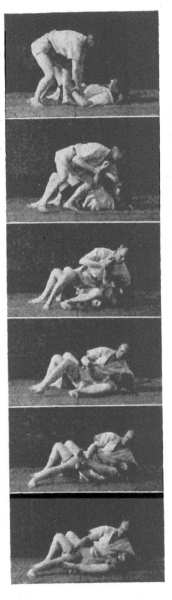

(3) THE HEEL AND THIGH STRAIGHT ARM LOCK

Stand at assailant's side as before; seize his left wrist with both hands and raise his arm about half-way, then release the grip of your left hand and place it flat on the mat close to the left side of your opponent's neck, to support your weight, whilst you slip your left thigh under his arm and sit down close to his armpit. (Phases I, II, and III.)

Press his arm down over your thigh and hold him round the neck with your left arm, at the same time raising your left foot and place it over his wrist, which should be palm uppermost. (Phases IV and V.)

Release the grip of your right hand as soon as you have got your foot over, and then press your foot down on his wrist, and press up against his elbow with your thigh, thus giving you the lock. (Phase VI.)

Lean your head well down so as to keep your weight well to one side and prevent him from rolling you over.

(4) THE CRADLE

Your assailant is lying flat on his back, and you are sitting by his left side, close to his left armpit, with your left arm round his throat and your left thigh under his left upper arm, one of the standard hold-down positions.

Slip your right arm under his nearest leg, so that the crook of your elbow hooks in to the crook of his knee. Place your hands on your thighs, the right hand on the right thigh and the left hand on the left thigh. Hook your hands round your thighs, and by closing your legs bring your opponent's head towards his knee, thus bringing a great pressure on his breast-bone and compelling him to submit.

Several tricks may be attempted from this hold-down position, but the above trick is usually attempted when your opponent has his arms round your body, thus preventing you from getting an arm lock.

This trick may be prevented, if done in time, by placing your left hand on the top of his head, and pressing his chin into his chest, or you may place your right hand on his forehead and pull his head back and pull him right over you.

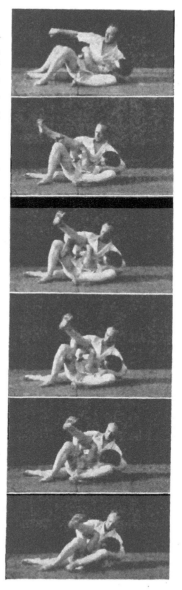

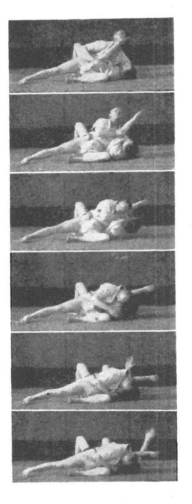

(5) THE SIDE NECK LOCK

Your assailant is lying flat on his back, and you are sitting by his left side, as in method No. 4.

Your opponent places his left hand on your chin, with the intention of trying to force you away and pushing you over his body to escape.

Raise your right hand, and give his elbow a vigorous push across your left shoulder and to the side of his neck.

Quickly take your hand away, and press your neck against his arm. Take hold of your left hand, and squeeze his neck against your forearm. The pressure of your forearm against his neck should be on the carotid artery, just below and in a line with his ear.

You should not keep this pressure on long, as, if you do, your opponent will quickly lose consciousness before he can give the signal of defeat.

(6) THE FURTHER BENT ARM LOCK

You are in the standard position, leaning across your assailant's chest with your knees on the mat at one side of him, and your arms on the other side. (Phase I.)

Take hold of his right wrist with your right hand, and slip your left arm under his upper arm, until you can grasp your own right wrist with your left hand, with your back upward. (Phase II.)

Now hold his right wrist firmly down on the mat with your right hand, and raise his elbow with your left arm, twisting his arm until he gives the signal of submission.

Practise this an equal number of times on the other side by transposing the movements above described.

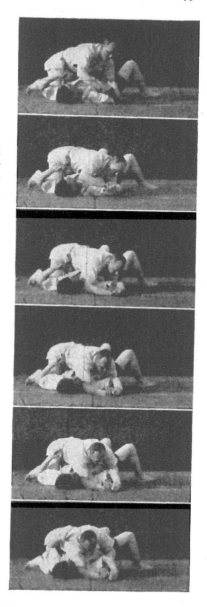

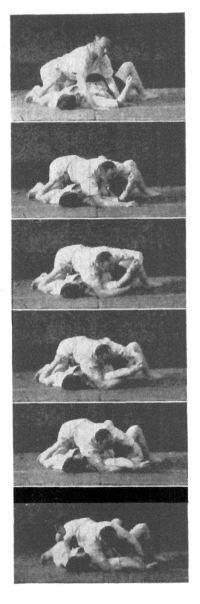

(7) THE FURTHER STRAIGHT ARM LOCK

Your assailant is lying flat on his back, and you are kneeling by his left side, with your knees well spread, as in method No. 6.

Your opponent's right arm is stretched out on the mat. Take hold of his right wrist with your left hand, the back of your hand uppermost and your opponent's wrist inside up.

Now slip your right forearm under his elbow joint, and place your right hand, back uppermost, on your own left wrist, then press his wrist down on the mat, at the same time bringing an upward pressure under his elbow joint with your right forearm and tensing the muscles of both your forearms.

Bring the pressure on firmly, but not with a jerk, until your opponent gives the signal of defeat, when you must instantly release him.

The above lock may be attempted when, after trying to get the Bent Arm Lock, your opponent forces his arm straight.

(8) THE TRUSSED ARM LOCK

You are in the standard position, leaning across your assailant's chest, with your knees on the mat at one side of him, and your arms on the other side. (Phase I.)

Your opponent's right arm is near his side on the mat. Take hold of his right wrist with your left hand, slip your right arm under his upper arm, and take an additional grip with your right hand on his right wrist. (Phase II.)

Now lever his right elbow up, and force his hand along his back up the spine, by raising your body and straightening your right arm. (Phase III.)

Continue this movement and place your left hand upon his elbow joint, giving it a downward pressure until he submits. (Phases IV and V.)

Practise this an equal number of times on the other side by transposing the movements above described.

(9) THE SPLITS

You are in the standard position astride your assailant, who is lying flat on his back on the mat. Your knees are on the mat, and your hands on his jacket collar. (Phase I.)

Place your hands flat on the mat, one on each side of your opponent, getting your weight on your arms and lowering your body. (Phase II.)

Slip your feet in between his legs, and hook your feet round his ankles, still lowering your body. (Phase III.)

Now straighten your legs and spread them apart as much as possible, at the same time raising your body to arm's length, and you will have a great strain upon your opponent's hip joints. (Phases IV and V.)

The counter for this lock is to lift your legs and straighten them the instant you conceive your opponent's intentions.

(10) THE HEAD LOCK

You are in the standard position astride your assailant, who is lying flat on his back on the mat. Your knees are on the mat, and your hands are on his jacket collar. (Phase I.)

Your opponent has raised his head, to prevent you from getting the collar hold. Place your left hand on the back of his head, keeping your weight well forward. (Phase II).

Quickly place your right hand over your left hand, and pull his chin in on to his chest. (Phase III.)

Continue pulling his head with both hands until he submits. (Phase IV.)

You can prevent this lock by not raising the head, as there is nothing to be gained by so doing, as you counter the collar hold another way.

H

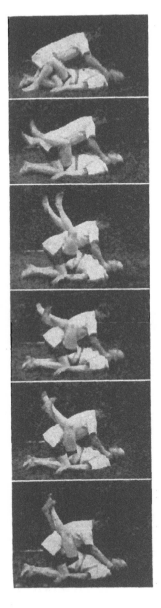

(II) THE KIDNEY SQUEEZE

You are lying flat on your back on the mat, and your assailant is kneeling on the mat between your legs, with his hands on your throat. (Phase I.)

Raise your hips and legs until your knees come just above his hip-bones. (Phases II and III.)

Cross your ankles, locking your feet and bending your legs slightly to enable you to do this. (Phase IV.)

Now straighten your legs, bracing well the muscles, and squeeze your opponent's body just above the hips as hard as you can until he submits. (Phase V.)

[NOTE.—It is a very bad position to get into, i.e. between your opponent's legs, and the experienced Jujitsuan always takes good care to avoid this. However, a novice often gets into this position.

A good way out is to dig your elbows into his thighs, or to reach behind and slip one of your arms in between his legs from above, and lift his leg up and over your head, immediately getting into one of the standard positions.]

(12) THE FIRST LEG LOCK

Your assailant is lying flat on his back on the mat, endeavouring to keep you away with his legs. Quickly seize one of his ankles. In the pictures it happens to be the left one. (Phase I.)

Slip your right arm round his ankle, securing it under your armpit, and get your weight on your right leg. (Phase II.)

Raise your left leg, pass it over his left leg, place your foot on the mat close to his left hip. (Phases III and IV.)

Bend your right leg and sink down close to the heel, and then on to your haunches, raising your left leg, which you place firmly on his chest to prevent him rising; then throw yourself back on to your shoulder-blades, and place your right foot on his left upper arm; hold your jacket lapel with your right arm, and arch your back, bringing a great strain upon the muscle just under his calf. (Phases V and VI.)

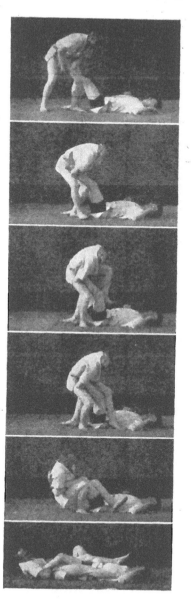

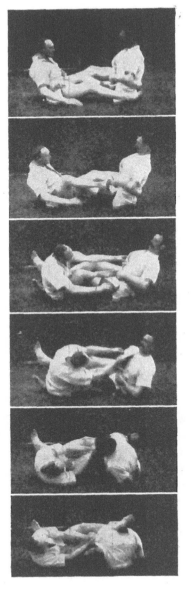

(13) GUARD AND COUNTER FOR FIRST LEG LOCK

Your assailant is attempting to obtain the First Leg Lock upon you.

He has secured the left leg under his armpit, and is about to throw himself back to complete the lock. (Phase I.)

Quickly raise your right leg and slip your foot under his right leg, at the same time reaching forward and grasping the lapel of his jacket. (Phases II, III, and IV.)

Roll on your right side, straightening your right leg, pull your opponent towards you as much as possible, and you will have the lock upon his right leg. (Phases V and VI.)

(14) THE SECOND LEG LOCK

Your assailant is lying flat
on his back on the mat.
Quickly kneel on the mat at
his right side, with your left
knee and your back turned
slightly towards his face.
(Phase I.)

Bend forward and slip your
left arm under his right knee,
and grasp the toes of his right
foot with your right hand.
(Phases II and III.)

Straighten your body, raising his leg and bringing your
left forearm under the soleus
muscle just below his calf.
(Phases IV and V.)

Place your left hand on your
right wrist and force his toes
downward, at the same time
pressing upward with your
left forearm. (Phase VI.)

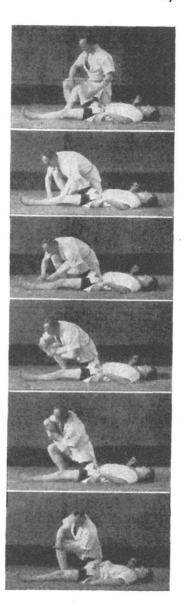

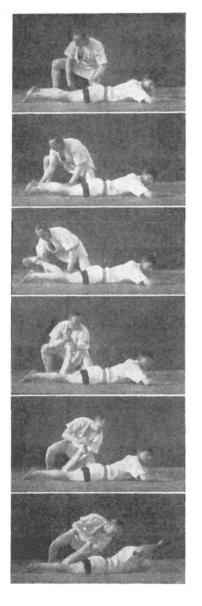

(15) THE THIRD LEG LOCK

Your assailant is lying flat on his chest on the mat, and you are kneeling on the mat at his left side on your left knee, with your back turned slightly towards his head. (Phase I.)

Bend forward and place your left hand on the top of his left knee, and grasp his left toes with your right hand. (Phase II.)

Raise the lower part of his left leg, pressing hard with your left hand on his knee, bring his leg up and over your left hand, and then force his foot down towards his haunches as far as possible. (Phases III, IV, and V.)

In Phase VI you will observe your opponent giving the signal of submission.

(16) THE FOURTH LEG LOCK

Your assailant is lying flat on his chest on the mat, and you are standing on the mat at his left side, with your back turned slightly towards his head. (Phase I.)

Bend your body forward and reach down and seize his left ankle with both hands, at the same time raising your left leg and placing your left foot in the crook of his left knee. (Phases II and III.)

Press hard on his left leg with your left foot, and pull up on his left ankle, shifting your right hand to his toes, which you take a firm grip of. (Phases IV and V.)

Force his leg over your foot, and then downward towards his haunches, and you will have a very effective leg lock. In the picture you will observe the opponent raising his hand ready to give the signal of submission. (Phase VI.)

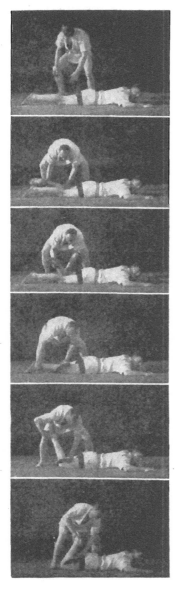

(17) THE FIFTH LEG LOCK

Your assailant is lying flat on his chest on the mat, and you are standing on the mat at his left side with your back turned slightly towards his head. (Phase I.)

Bend forward and reach down, placing your left hand on the inside of his knee, and your right hand under his left ankle. (Phase II.)

Lift the lower part of his left leg, still pressing hard on his knee with your left hand, and place his ankle in the crook of his right knee, then quickly seize his right ankle with your right hand. (Phases II, III, and IV.)

Lift the lower part of his right leg and force it over his left ankle, slipping your right hand to his toes, then press his right foot hard down towards his haunches, thus securing the Fifth Leg Lock. (Phases V and VI.)

(18) THE SIXTH LEG LOCK

Your assailant is on the mat on his hands and knees, similar to a wrestler's position in the Catch-as-catch-can style, and you are behind him, stooping down to seize his right ankle. (Phase I.)

Seize his right ankle with both hands, and pull his leg up until his foot reaches your waist, then step over his leg with your left leg. (Phases II and III.)

Place your left foot down on the mat on the other side of his leg, and bring his right ankle under your left armpit. (Phases IV and V.)

Now leave go his ankle, turn your chest towards your opponent's back, and lean forward, pressing your waist against his shin and forcing his leg over on to his haunches, thus securing the lock. In the last picture you will observe the opponent with his right hand raised, about to give the signal of submission. (Phase VI.)

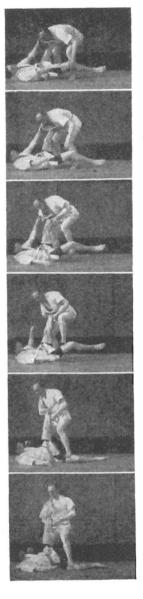

(19) THE SEVENTH LEG LOCK

Your assailant is lying flat on his back on the mat, after being thrown by the Inside Ankle Trip.

Pull your assailant's left leg under your right armpit, pressing his right knee down with your left hand. (Phase I.)

Get your weight well on your right leg, and grip your right fist in your left hand. (Phases II and III.)

Place your left foot on your opponent's right thigh, to prevent him kicking you or using his legs to throw you, then straighten up your body and press upward strongly with your right forearm under his leg muscle, and you will have the Seventh Leg Lock. (Phases IV, V, and VI.)

This leg lock may be attempted at any time when you are near your opponent's legs and he is trying to keep you away from his body or to throw you.

CHAPTER V
Ground Manœuvres

(1) THE STRAIGHT ARM LOCK FROM ASTRIDE

Your assailant is lying flat on his back, and you are in the standard position astride with your knees on the mat. (Phase I.)

Your opponent stretches out his left arm, and pushes your chin with his hand. (Phase II.)

Seize his left wrist with your right hand, turning your body to your left. (Phase III.)

Place your left hand flat on the mat, and raise your right leg. (Phase IV.)

Place your right foot down on the mat, so that your leg comes under his chin, and force his left elbow joint against the inside of your right thigh, thus obtaining a very effective arm lock. (Phases V and VI.)

(2) ESCAPING FROM STANDARD POSITION ASTRIDE

You are lying flat on your back on the mat, and your assailant is in the standard astride position over you, with one knee on each side of you on the mat, and attempting to obtain the Collar Hold. (Phase I.)

Place your right hand in the crook of his left elbow, and your left hand on his right hip. (Phase II.)

Pull down strongly on his elbow, push round to your right on his hip with your left hand, and roll your body round to your right, thus throwing your opponent over on to his back on your right side. (Phases IV and V.)

Continue to roll to your right until you are on your knees, then rise on your opponent's left side, where you can follow with the Straight Arm Lock between Thighs, described and illustrated in the next method. (Phase VI.)

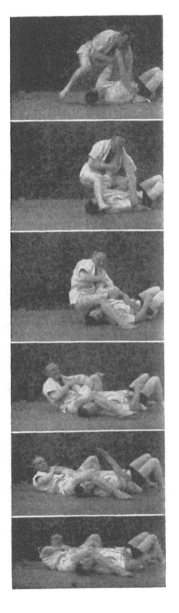

(3) SECURING ARM LOCK AFTER ESCAPING ASTRIDE

You have escaped from your assailant's standard position astride you, described in the previous method, and are now at his left side, grasping his left wrist with your right hand. (Phase I.)

Sink down on your left leg and circle your right leg round and over his head, and then across his throat, quite close to his armpit. (Phases II and III.)

Sink down on to your haunches and then on to your shoulder-blades, pulling his arm along your body, and then over your left thigh, pressing his wrist down towards the mat on your left side. (Phases IV, V, and VI.)

In Phases V and VI you can plainly observe the opponent giving the signal of defeat by tapping his right hand on the mat.

(4) ESCAPING FROM STAND-
ARD POSITION KNEELING

You are lying flat on your
back on the mat, and your
assailant is in the standard
position, kneeling at your
left side with his chest
across yours, and en-
deavouring to obtain an arm
lock upon your right arm.
(Phase I.)

Place your left hand
under his right armpit, and
push your opponent over
your body towards your
right side, in a slanting
direction, at the same time
rolling your body over to
your right. (Phases II, III,
and IV.)

Continue to push him
over you and on to his
shoulder-blades, at the
same time rolling your
body round to your right,
and placing your right forearm down on the mat to
assist you to rise. (Phase V.)

Now rise to your feet,
where your can attempt an
arm lock, or get into one
of the standard positions.

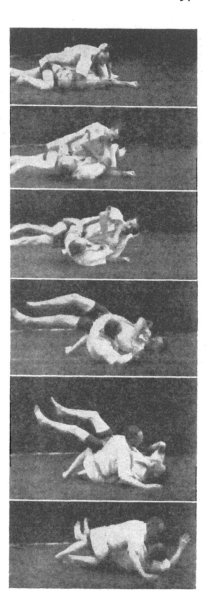

(5) ESCAPING FROM STANDARD
POSITION SITTING

You are lying flat on your back on the mat, and your assailant is in the standard position, sitting on the mat on your right side with his right arm round your throat, trying to obtain the Heel and Thigh Arm Lock. (Phase I.)

Place your arms round your opponent's waist just above the hips, and turn your body a little to your right, getting your stomach as close to his back as possible. (Phase II.)

Now grip your adversary firmly round the body, and roll him completely over you to your left side. (Phases III and IV.)

Continue the roll of your body and rise to your feet, or get the Standard Position Astride. Phase VI shows the act of rising after escaping.

(6) THE USE OF THE LEGS IN ESCAPING

You are lying flat on your back on the mat, and your assailant is kneeling on the mat near your feet, leaning over your body, trying to throttle you. (Phase I.)

Place your left foot under your opponent's right knee in the crook and your left hand on his right elbow. (Phase II.)

Place your right hand on his left jacket sleeve, and commence to lift him over with your left leg. (Phase III.)

Continue turning your opponent over until he is on his back, then throw your left leg over him and rise to the Standard Position Astride, where you can attempt one of several methods to gain submission. (Phases IV, V, and VI.)

(7) ARM LOCK FROM UNDER POSITION

You are lying flat on your back on the mat, and your assailant is kneeling on the mat between your legs, with his left hand clutching at your throat, and his right arm raised to strike. (Phase I.)

Seize your assailant's left wrist with both your hands, and place the sole of your left foot against his right hip. (Phase II.)

Push your assailant's hip away strongly with your foot, and swing your right leg over his head and your leg under his chin. (Phases III and IV.)

Roll your body round to your left, push your opponent down on to his right side, and take an additional grip on his wrist with your right hand. (Phase V.)

Now press your right thigh strongly against his elbow joint, at the same time pressing his arm back to your right, and you will have the arm lock. (Phase VI.)

(8) LEG LOCK FROM UNDER POSITION

You are lying flat on your back on the mat, and your assailant is kneeling over you with his right leg between your legs, his knee on the mat and his hands on your throat. (Phase I.)

Raise your left leg and pass it over his right leg, then slip your left foot under his right ankle, and place your right foot under his ankle, so that it comes between your left instep and his right foot. (Phases II, III, and IV.)

Now straighten your legs, bringing a great strain upon his ankle joint and thus obtaining the leg lock. In the last phase you will observe the opponent giving the signal of submission with his right hand.

This can be done on the other side, if your opponent gets his left leg between your legs. All you have to do is to transpose your movements.

CHAPTER VI

Jujitsu versus Boxing

(1) DEFENCE FOR LEFT LEAD AT FACE (A)'

As your assailant leads off at your face with his left fist, guard his blow by raising your right forearm, bringing it under his wrist in an upward and outward direction, and with the palm of your hand away from you. (Phases I and II.)

Quickly place your left hand upon his left shoulder, draw your right heel up to your left heel, getting your weight well on your right leg and turning your right hand farther round away from you, and seize his wrist in a firm grip. (Phase III.)

Now raise your left leg, bring it behind your opponent's left leg on the outside, and give the back of his left knee a sharp jab, at the same time pulling round on his wrist, pushing on his shoulder, and throwing him flat on his back in front of you, where you may follow up with an arm lock. (Phases IV, V, and VI.)

In the last phase you will observe that the opponent is about to break his fall with his right hand. Also that he has been knocked completely off his feet.

(2) DEFENCE FOR LEFT LEAD
AT FACE (B)

Guard your assailant's blow with your left forearm by raising your arm with the palm of your hand turned away from you, and ward off the blow in an upward and outward direction to your left. (Phases I and II.)

Turn the palm of your left hand farther round and seize his wrist in a firm grip, then lower his arm, at the same time twisting it round so that his elbow joint faces upward, and make a wide step backward with your left leg, turning your body to your left. (Phases III and IV.)

Now place your right forearm upon his elbow joint, press down strongly, at the same time pulling up on his wrist with your left hand, and you will have the lock. (Phases V and VI.)

In the last phase you will observe the opponent about to give the signal of submission with his right hand.

(3) DEFENCE FOR LEFT LEAD AT FACE (SCISSORS) (C)

Your assailant is shaping up in the orthodox boxing position, and aims a blow at your face. (Phase I.)

Turn slightly to your left, and quickly place your hands down flat on the mat near your left foot, bringing your right leg slightly to the front of your left leg. (Phases II to IV.)

Throw up your legs so that your right leg goes across your opponent's thighs, and your left leg goes across the back of his knees. (Phase V.)

Now throw yourself round on to your shoulder-blades, and your opponent will be thrown over backward. (Phase VI.)

The breakfall for this throw is to beat the mat with both hands before the shoulders touch, as explained at the beginning of this book.

(4) DEFENCE FOR LEFT LEAD AT FACE (D)

As your assailant leads off at your face with his left fist, duck your head to your left, so that his blow goes over your right shoulder, at the same time throwing your right arm round his body, and placing your left hand in the crook of his right elbow, to prevent his giving you a blow with his right fist. (Phases I, II, and III.)

Step forward in front of his legs with your right leg, slip your hips well under him, and catch hold of his elbow over the joint with your left arm. (Phases IV and V.)

Now lurch forward with a twist of your body to your right, at the same time straightening your legs, and throw him over your right hip to the mat in front of you. (Phase VI.)

(5) DEFENCE FOR LEFT LEAD AT MARK

Your assailant leads off at your 'mark' with his left fist. Immediately make a downward and outward guard with your right forearm which should come in contact with his wrist, then quickly place your left hand on the top of his elbow joint so that your fingers pass over and round the bones. (Phases I and II.)

Pull his elbow sharply towards you, at the same time slipping your right arm under his left arm until you can place your right hand on his left shoulder. As you do this you must turn your body round to your left so that you face the same direction as your assailant. (Phases III to V.)

Now place your right leg in front of your assailant's left leg, pull down strongly on his elbow with your left fingers and lever up his forearm with your right arm, and you will have the Trussed Arm Lock. (Phase VI.)

In Phase V you will observe that the assailant is in the act of giving the signal of defeat.

(6) DEFENCE FOR RIGHT BLOW AT FACE (HIP-THROW)

Guard your assailant's blow with his right fist at your face with your left forearm by raising your arm in front of your face, and then weaving it to your left. (Phases I and II.)

Immediately after guarding, turn the palm of your hand towards his arm and catch his wrist, then throw your right arm round his neck, at the same time stepping forward with your right leg, and slipping your hips under him, bending well at the knees; then straighten your legs and bend forward with a slight twist sideways, and throw him completely over your hips to the mat. (Phases III to VI.)

After the throw you can, of course, attempt an arm lock, or sit down with your back to him and obtain the Heel and Thigh Straight Arm Lock described in Chapter IV, method No. 3.

Your opponent must break the fall with his left arm and both feet, bending well at the knees.

(7) ANOTHER DEFENCE FOR RIGHT BLOW AT FACE

Guard your assailant's right blow at your face by crossing your wrists, the left wrist undermost with the palm of the hand turned towards you, and the back of your right hand towards you. (Phase I.)

Make a quick right-about turn, seizing his wrist with both hands at the same time, and turning the inside of his wrist uppermost. (Phase II.)

Slip your left shoulder under his elbow joint, and then pull down on his wrist, thus giving you a very powerful arm lock. (Phases III to VI.)

The lock should be brought on very carefully, as if it is done with a jerk serious injury may easily result.

(8) DEFENCE FOR RIGHT LEAD AT
SHORT RIBS

As your assailant leads off at your short ribs with his right fist, guard the blow with your left forearm, bringing your arm down and raising your elbow and deflecting the blow to your left. (Phases I and II.)

Quickly seize his right wrist with your right hand, the palm of your hand coming on the inside of his wrist. (Phase III.)

Turn your body to your right, drawing his arm under your armpit, wrapping your left arm round over his upper arm and your forearm under his elbow joint. (Phases IV and V.)

Now place your left hand on your right wrist, press down strongly on his wrist with your right hand, and press upward under his elbow joint with your left forearm. You will then have the arm lock. (Phase VI.)

This arm lock is exactly the same as the Come Along Arm Lock. In the case of an assailant with a longer arm than yourself, you should hold your jacket instead of your wrist.

Lightning Source UK Ltd.
Milton Keynes UK
UKHW010056300422
402273UK00001B/404